Of Yesteryear

Lauren Eden

ISBN-13: 978-0646951867
ISBN-10: 0646951866

"Mais où sont
les neiges d'antan?"

- François Villon
Ballade des dames du temps jadis, Le Testament

CONTENTS

ALL WE CANNOT SAY

We live
in the small
spaces
between
our words

hiding
between
the said

and all
we cannot
say.

UNIVERSE

His mind
is a universe.

I could
lie down
on his bed
for hours
just listening
to him talk

watching
the words
fall from
his mouth
like stars.

ARCH

Nothing
betrays me
more

than
the arch
in my back

leaning away
from you

when I
want you
most.

LOSING YOU

The sky
tore in half
like an old
bedsheet-

each star
falling
between
the gap

disappearing

until
there was
no light
left.

NOT ONE

I walk
into a room

and there
is not one
person
I want
to talk to

except
for the guy
who wants
to take me
back to his

and not
talk to me.

TOO BIG AN ASK

Just
his hand
resting lightly
on the small
of my back
feels too big
an ask.

SOMEONE ELSE

We shifted
so far
to the opposite
sides of
the bed
we made
room
for
someone
else
to slip
between us.

METAMORPHOSIS

I hide my wings from you.

I'm so ashamed
to have changed
while you have stayed
the same

and I am trying
my hardest to stay
in this cocoon with you

but I can feel
something
shifting in me-

a small fire
in my belly
spreading
to my toes

hands
that fly away
from me
like birds

my heart
a changing moon.

I fear my metamorphosis
has come too soon.

RESOLVE

I'm not sure
our resolve
is proven
in our highs
and in our lows

but in all
the days
in between

where nothing
much happens.

KALEIDOSCOPE

He is
my kaleidoscope
of desire.

A thousand
different ways-

only him.

MOST

I knew
I loved him
most

when I
knew that
it was he

I wanted
to hurt
least.

TIDAL WHISPERS

I breathe you in

you breathe me out

like tidal whispers
slithering about.

Inhaling and exhaling
sailing to shore-

I cannot quite tell
who is who anymore.

TOO LITTLE

He
is too
little
of too
much
I need.

FEELINGS

Sometimes
I think
it would be
easier
to steal
the sky
from night
like a blanket

and shake out
all the stars
like dust

than
it would be

to get
some feelings
out of you.

THAT TYPE OF GIRL

I am
that type
of girl

that makes
men want to
pull their hair out
in frustration

and mine
in lust-

both
at the same
time.

ALONE

He tells me
I will end up
alone

and I tell him
but we all do.

Just sometimes
it is our doing

and sometimes
it is not.

THE WORLD IN YOU

I will remember
the slope
of your neck
curved and white
like a crescent moon
more than I will
the moon

the pink
of my palms
folding into you
more than
my hands in prayer

the burn
of your eyes
more than
the sun

tracks
of your touch
more than
the places I'd go

and kisses
more than stars-
(kisses always
more than stars).

The truth is
I had the world
in you

and when you
ended

it did too.

EVERYTHING I TOUCH

I burnt
my hands
in his flame

and now
everything
I touch

hurts
like him.

MY OTHER LOVERS

You may
awaken
my other
lovers
buried
in the
memory
of my skin
as you
love me.

Make me
forget them.

VEILS

Even
our skin
felt like
it was
getting
in the way
of us.

LIFE

Life
is just
a window
I poke
my head
in and
out of
between
daydreams.

RAIN

Don't
tell me
you love
the rain

when you
don't stay
to watch
her dry

after
she's fallen
for you.

WHAT SHE DOESN'T KNOW

He still
tells me
he misses me

but he
is considerate
enough
to tell me
when she
is sleeping

to not wake
her suspicions.

IMPOSSIBLY

I was
quite
possibly
impossibly
in love
with him.

SCATTER

I just
love him.

That is
all I know
and will
ever know.

Whichever way
the wind
blows

my heart
will not
scatter.

I SPIED

I spied
love
in the
blinks
of his
eyes

but he
swears
he never
saw
a thing.

CUSP

I am
balancing
delicately
on the cusp
of wanting you
and needing you-

that line I scratch
so deeply in the dust
is unsettling
as I am in myself

with every part
of me standing
on end for you

begging
upon your hands
to be laid
flat.

JOURNEY

How far
I must've
strayed
to feel
such
a journey
in coming
home
to myself.

REINS

You need
to control
your feelings
for me.

She thinks
they are
hers.

NO OTHER YOU

I will
shake
the world
trying to
find you
again

and out
will fall stars
as alike
as the next

but there
will be
no other you-

there is
no other
you.

TUG OF WAR

I play
tug of war
with the universe
to keep you.

MEMORY LANE

I trip down
memory lane

and fall back
into your arms

every time.

MAGIC

I am magic.

I can turn
just one night
with me
into
the rest
of your life

if you only
believe
in me.

YOUR DISAPPOINTMENTS

Your
disappointments
don't
make me
question
my ability
to please you.

They
make me
question
your ability
to be pleased.

INSANITY

I am
always
surprised
when
someone
hurts me

no matter
how many times
I've been
hurt before

and I can't
seem to
work out

if that
is the definition
of innocence

or insanity.

LOVE

I just
wish love
was something
you were
good at.

FOOTSTEPS

We stay
longer
than we
should.

We've
all said
far too many
goodbyes
in this life

we'd rather
leave the door
ajar
to hear
the sound
of footsteps.

BLUE MOON

Once
in a blue moon
you will find
magic
in a man

amongst
the unfinished
spells
and empty
potions

and he'll
let you
drink him

for the rest
of your
white moons.

YOURS

I am yours-

so effortlessly
yours.

Just
one look

and
I couldn't
be mine

if I tried.

WISHES

We are
wishes
that
come true

only
for the ones
who believe
in us.

MASTERPIECES

I try not
to forget
all the things
I loved

but wear them
on the inside

hanging up

like pictures
in a gallery
I can admire
in my quiet
moments
alone.

There is
art
in life

and it painted
such masterpieces
in me.

CHANGE OF HEART

Why
is it easier
for us

to accept
a mind's
change
of mind

than
a heart's
change
of heart?

THAT LITTLE VOICE

I didn't change.

I just learnt
some manners

by letting
that little voice
inside me speak

before it was
interrupted

with what
you wanted.

AWKWARD SILENCES

Awkward silences
are the naked flash
of a person
not ready
to be exposed

before they
quickly cover
themselves
back up
with words.

A FICKLE FANTASY

I am
just a girl
who is too little
for the love
you desire.

I can
make fires
but not
keep them.

I can
tend to
but cannot grow
the fruits
you seek.

I am
neither meek
nor mild-

I am
brash
and unkept

like your shirt
untucked-

yes, I noticed this.

Do you see
my plight within?

I will fall
out of love
with you

as quickly
as I fall in.

HURRICANE

I loved him
like a gentle
breeze

but I miss him
like a hurricane.

PLEASE

Please don't
make me stay
to watch
you
slowly
fall out
of love
with me.

LAST ATTEMPT

We both
know
that you
hurting me

is your last
attempt

to get me
to feel
something
for you.

ALL MY BROKEN THINGS

He
made me
want to fix
all my broken
things.

I didn't
want him
standing
in the rubble
of me

unable
to get close
enough.

HE TELLS ME THINGS

He tells me
things about
myself
I never knew

and I don't
know
whether
that means
he knows me
more than
I know myself

or that he
really doesn't
know me
at all.

CIRCLES

He drew
circles
in my palms
until
I couldn't
see straight.

THE BEST PARTS OF ME

I thought
he was
just dreaming
me up

but I was
the one
who'd been
sleeping
through
the best
parts
of me.

NOTHING ELSE

He looked
at me
like there
was nothing
else
needing
to be done.

LIKE A RECORD

Repeat it.

Tell me
you love me
again

over
and over

like a record
skipping.

Let my heart
get stuck
on your words

until
your voice
sounds like

short
deep beats

playing with
my heartbeat.

MORE THAN A GIRL'S BEST FRIEND

His eyes
were diamonds
I wore best
with nothing
else at all.

HER OWN NIGHT

The sun
makes
her own
night

shining
upon the sea
with her light
until it dazzles
like a galaxy
of stars

and
she smiles

knowing

she can do
anything
the moon can.

NAIVE

Keep me
naive
enough
to think

that a simple
pull of
the drapes
is enough
to keep
the world
outside

from
hurting me.

ALL THE ARMS

Dreams,

cover me
like a blanket

of all
the arms
I've ever felt
around me.

REGRETS

I awake
still paying
for last night's
sins

as I untangle you
from my legs
and pick
your words
from my teeth-

watching you
pick up
your things
off my things

listening
to the click
of the door
behind you
as I spit
myself out
like seeds-

sitting quietly
with my head
in my hands

waiting to grow
back again.

DAGGERS

He will
love you

and he
will hurt you-

it is inevitable.

But when
he hurts you

are his daggers
in his eyes

or in
your back?

NOT ME

I end up
disliking
everyone
in the end.

They are
not me

and that
is difficult
to accept.

FATE

Of all
the doors
in the universe…

and we
are in
the same
room.

EVERYTHING OF ME

Come to me
he says.

He reaches out
his hands

his fingertips
barely
skimming
my thighs

and I feel
everything
of me

part

to make
room
for him.

IN HIM

I could
live
in him

and forget
to look
through
his eyes

back at
the world.

A LOVE POEM

The world
feels quiet

like it's just
you and I

   shhh...

and maybe
that's how
it's supposed
to feel.

We love

and the world
gets smaller
and smaller

until
all the rooms
disappear

and leave
only one.

GREEDY

You hold
my hand
in yours

while
the other
hangs

sulkily

like
a sullen
child

who has
to wait
her turn
of you.

SECRETS

It's not
that I don't
trust you
with my
secrets-

I just
don't like
talking
about them
behind
their backs.

LIES

We judge
others
for living
a lie

when
the truth is

most of us
are dying
in them.

PLEASE DON'T

I need you
to not touch me.

Your hands
light on my hips
weigh me down
like sinking ships

and I would
rather drown
than take your hand-

we have been here before-

you must understand

how your touch
pulls all my wild horses
from the mire.

You know
I could never
be dragged from
your fire.

YOU JUST DON'T WANT TO BE LONELY

Not
wanting me
to leave

is not
the same

as wanting me
to stay.

BLINK

You say
the eyes
never lie.

You blink

and
I don't
believe you.

I LOVE YOU NOT

You
rip off
my petals

one by one

then
wonder why
the last one
you hold
tells you

that I love you

not.

TICKING CLOCK

I only like
the sound
of a ticking
clock
when you
leave me-

it is
your heartbeat

and I wait.

A PLACE THAT'S NOT ME

I need
to be
inside
of a place
that's
not me-

somewhere

where
no part
longer
knows you.

NEXT SUMMER

I planned
my escape
from him

while looking
dead into
his eyes
arranging
our next
Summer
vacation

knowing

there would
never
be another
Summer
between us

so do not
tell me

that we
ever really
know anyone
at all.

TOO SHY TO TELL YOU

You throw me
onto the bed
and I'm too shy
to tell you

that I'd like
to be folded
please

and tucked in
the sheets

like a letter
in an envelope

you take
the time
to read.

WHAT LOVE SHOULD DO

You just
don't do
what love
should do

and I
can love

though not
for you.

SLIP

I slip
out of
myself

and become
for him.

I know
what he
needs

and
sometimes
it's not
me.

HOW MANY NIGHTS

How many
nights
must we go
without

before
the boil
of yearning
starts to
evaporate
us?

DISAPPEARING ACTS

It was
clear to see

that
the only
magic
he was
going to
perform

was of
the disappearing
kind.

MISTAKEN IDENTITY

Men keep
tapping me
on the shoulder
and mistaking
me for Love

but she is
much prettier
than I am.

MY FAVOURITE COMPANY

The most
dangerous thing
about me
is that I am
my favourite
company.

You will
have to
fight me
for me.

I SAW THE STARS

I saw
the stars
squabbling
over
whose turn
it was
to shine
upon you
next.

TWO CAUGHT FISH

We were ships
in the night
passing through
our cool waters
of blue-

not even love
could anchor time.

And there
was God
scribbling
in his yellow notebook
on the jetty
in between bites

reeling in
two caught fish
on one hook
that looked
an awfully lot
like us

lured by the same bait

helpless
in fate's bucket
of ice.

ONCE

Once
he showed me
the world

I lost
my place
in it

and found
myself
only
in him.

YOUR HANDS

I remember
your hands-

I would never forget them.

Look closer
at the lines
inside your palms-

I wrote
all my love letters
to you
upon them.

CANDLES

I wish
I'd saved
all my
birthday
wishes.

He is what
I want most

and
I feel like
I'm running
out of candles.

TIME

He made
the hours
disappear

and the
minutes fade

until time
became

simply

when
he was
with me

and when
he was not.

ALL THE STARS

Don't tell me
I'll miss the moon-

the changing moon

and the stars
that twinkle in any
which mood.

Give me him
in a room
without a window

and you shall see
how soon my idols
become skin deep.

The man in the moon
can take a rain check-

my lover
is showing me
all the stars
I can bear tonight.

INDECISION

My heart
loved you
at first sight

but
my head

still

cannot
make up
its mind
about you.

SOME NIGHTS

There are
some nights

I would rather
lie down
in the graves
of my heartbreaks

than lie alone
in an empty bed.

TWO HANDS

Maybe
we were
given
two hands

so that we
may hold
our own

in the times
we do not
have another's
to hold.

POINTED FINGERS

Your
pointed fingers
at me
really did
end up
poking
too many
holes
in my love
for you.

I told you so.

HUM

It is not
the world
that tires
me so

but
the constant
hum
in my head
like bees
buzzing
manically

working
to create
more thoughts
into honey.

THE EVOLUTION OF MAN

Men
wear hearts
on the sleeves
that boys wipe
their noses on.

CONFUSION

I do not find
confusion
confusing
at all.

In fact
it may
just be
the only
thing
in this life

I have ever
understood.

STEADFAST

A tree
proves
its strength
quietly

standing
steadfast
in one place

while we
walk
in circles.

WADING

I'm not falling
in love-

I'm wading
in it.

Dipping
in my toes
but not
my knees-

I like them
strong
and unbuckled

like my men.

MY ALMOST

He was my almost

but he
had moons
for eyes
that changed
with the flavour
of his drink.

He'd cup
my face
in his hands
like a vase
and call me
his Lily

but all
flowers die-
even with
the sun's
giving gaze
upon them.

They need
more to live

and I needed more
than the almost love
he could give me.

BROKEN

He holds
his arms
around me

while mine
hang flat
and still
to my sides
like the broken
wings of a bird
unable to fly

but yield-

leaning
into him
like there
is nothing
else left
to do.

BAD TASTE

I wake up
with a bad taste
in my mouth
from all the words
of love I said
the night before
that weren't true.

I was lonely

just like you.

LOVE SCALES

I just
want to feel
more love
when we
love

than hurt
when we
hurt.

PLEASE DON'T BE EVERYTHING

Please
don't be
everything
I've ever
wanted-

I may
just forget
how to be
anything
to myself.

CRAWL

He made
my skin
crawl
to you.

HEALER

He put
his hands
on me

and I
could feel
every hurt
I'd ever felt
unbury themselves

rising to
the surface
of my skin

to be touched
by him.

HIS

I am mine
in the daylight hours

until I grow
too heavy in me

and that
is when
he takes over
for the night

and makes me
his.

PEDESTRIAN LOVE

He crossed
my mind
and kept
walking.

MINE

I will
make you
forget
that your
hands
ever
belonged
to you.

INSTINCT

I will laugh
at them
when they
tell me
I had
a choice.

I never had a choice.

I saw him
and there I was.

LAYERS OF YOU

I am
wrapped up
so tightly
in love

I forget
that they
are my bones
underneath
all those
layers
of you.

LULLABIES

I sing
lullabies
to my fears.

After all

they are
just children

who grew up
too quickly.

FEMINIST

Do I like men?

Yes.

I just like
to make
love
to them

more
than I like
to love them.

WINDOWS

Do not tell me
who I am
before I know.

That is impossible-

I live in me.

It's like saying
you have lived
in a house

when you've
only peeked
through its
windows.

PICK YOU

Run for the hills
and keep running

farther and farther
until all the people
you once loved
are just tiny dots
of colour

like flowers
you dare not
pick again

but pick you.

Always pick you.

MARGIN

We
have all
had that
one love

just outside
the margin
of our ruled
pages

hiding
to the left
of our focus

not quite
right enough
to be centred.

REVOLVING DOOR

My revolving
door swings
and in walks
a different
version
of you.

WRONG

I'm trying
so hard
to be right
for you
I'm becoming
wrong

so wrong

for me.

BEHIND OUR BACKS

We try
to love
with
our hands
behind
our backs

so we
can just
lean in
and take
what we need

without
holding on.

MY BEST PAGES

Time
turns all
my best
pages
before
I've finished
reading them.

MELANCHOLIA

I would stroke
sleep until
she slept

and make hurt
cry until
he wept.

I would make
grief grieve
a lonely death

and honesty ask
for truth
in an empty
church pew.

Let the prayers
pray

let my days
and my nights
wish for you.

My tiredness
is getting tired

and my love
is out of
love.

SHINY

How long
do I need
to close
my eyes
until
my life
looks shiny
again?

TEAPOT

I may not be
your cup of tea

but that
doesn't mean
you should tell
the teapot
I shouldn't
be poured.

DEAD SKIN

I shed people
like dead skin
I've worn
too long.

Some people
feel too
heavy on me

and how am I
to carry
what I cannot
carry?

ROSEMARY

I can recite
most of our
conversations
as I can
the works
of Plath
and Wilde.

The long ago
of you
and the small
nova you burnt
into my darkness
made you
an instant classic
without the library
to back it up-

just one book
with its dog-eared
corners and twigs
of rosemary
pressed inside
its pages-

the way
I wish you
were still
pressed
inside
of me.

GRAVES

I sleep
in the graves
of every
person
that ever
left me.

TOO BADLY

I want you
too badly
for you
to ever
be good
for me.

OLIVE BRANCH

I graciously
accepted
his olive branch

but I knew
from then on
I would
always find
the smell
of olives

nauseating.

DEAD IN THE WATER

Dead
in the water-

our love

drowned

sunk

masquerading junk
fooling
as treasure.

HEARTBREAK

He looked like love

until he got closer.

Then he
just looked
like heartbreak.

HURT

I hurt people.

And that
is how
I know

I am not
immune
to it.

A SECRET THIS GOOD

You are
a secret
the world
will inevitably
find out.

No one
can keep
a secret
this good.

COVERS

Who I am
beneath
the covers
is not
who I am
between them.

MY SOLITUDE

It is tiring
to hold on
to my solitude

like a blanket
being pulled
away
by all these
frantic hands

begging
for warmth.

CENTREPIECE

You are
the centrepiece
in my mind

making all
my other
thoughts jealous

as they sulkily
take their seats
around you.

A NOTE TO LOVE

Just for
a moment

let me
hold you
Love

and let me
believe

that I
can be
the one

to keep you
still.

DIRECTIONS

His fingers
mapped
all the places
he wanted
his mouth
to go

and I didn't
dare question
a man
and his
directions.

STAND TALL

They try
to put books
on our heads

when we
just want
to read them.

HOW MANY LIVES

How
many lives
does our
love have
before
we need
to bury us
and mourn
our ghosts
of almost?

FANTASIES

You
fascinate
my fantasies-

even they
could not
conjure

the magic
of you.

THIS IS WHY I PLAY THESE GAMES

Our love
has become
so quiet

that the only time
I can hear it

is when
I leave you.

MY WORDS

I wish
I could've
caught
my words
before
they flew
into his ears

like butterflies

down into
the cocoon
of his mind-

I fear
what they
may become
on the other
side.

BEAUTY MAGAZINES

They have
too much
to say
about
the bodies
we had
no say in.

COMPANY

It's not
that you
haven't found
the right
company-

it's that
you have
never
felt right
in yours.

GLASS JAR

I could
swim
in a glass jar

and he
would
make me
believe

it was
the ocean.

PEACE

Peace
will feel

like
everybody
I have
ever hurt

smiling
back at me

again.

BLUE MURDER

His eyes
are killing me-

blue murder.

Shooting me
with his black
pupil bullets

his starburst iris

his ghostly whites

and I am
his victim

planning
my escape

as he blinks.

WHAT MY HEART DOESN'T

I'm scared
of what
my heart
wants

but
I'm scared
mostly

by what
it doesn't.

ROOM

I used to walk
into a room
and expect
to turn heads.

Now
I just walk
into a room

and expect
to walk
into a room.

I ONLY KNEW LOVE

I only
knew love
like the back
of my hand
when it was
inside his.

THEY DON'T UNDERSTAND

He is
the brick
through
my window.

All they see
is the shattered
glass

and all I see
is the light
being let in.

A MAN'S JOB

I am
asking a boy
to do
a man's job
and love me.

SUNDAY

On
a Sunday
he left me.

They were
on their knees
praying
to God
in church

while
I was
at his feet

begging him

to believe
in me.

Of Yesteryear is Lauren Eden's first published poetry collection. She also shares her writing on her Instagram account of the same name @ofyesteryear

14461033R00102

Printed in Poland
by Amazon Fulfillment
Poland Sp. z o.o., Wrocław